ON

MARKETING

BLACK RAGE

Editions Canaan

ON MARKETING BLACK RAGE

To Paula and André Kabeya

ON MARKETING BLACK RAGE

VKY -Victoria Kabeya- is a French-Belgian author, poetess and essayist of African and Middle Eastern descent. She was born in 1991. After she obtained her Master's Degree in English, she began her career as a writer in 2015. She has now published more than twenty books and is also an occasional journalist. Her books have been translated in English, Italian and Portuguese.

Photo credits: FromJaipur/ Ibtissem

ON MARKETING BLACK RAGE

The Black complex of heroism

On the Black French mentality

There, a distinction should be made. The Black French community also called «diaspora africaine de France» should be divided into two separate and distinct groups. The first one is mostly constituted by West Indians -from Martinique, Guadeloupe or even French Guyana- and Africans with roots in West and Central Africa whose countries were colonized by France for a century. The two groups became a majority but can not be compared on a political level.

Indeed, the West Indians have proven to be the most coherent, united, efficient and organized of them all. The descendants of slaves and living under French colonial rule ever since, they have provided France with prolific intellectual and cultural individuals such as Aimé Césaire, Maryse Condé, Alexandre Dumas, Juliette Smeralda, Frantz Fanon or even Guyanese Christiane Taubira, responsible for the 2001 bill which led to slavery being recognized as a crime against humanity. Though imperfect, the community has heavily contributed to the advancement of Black issues. Yet, they remain marginalized by the French Metropolitan media, their social issues being related to the colonial treatment they were granted and later replaced by the wave of African refugees who migrated in the late 1990s and 2000s. Contrary to the French Africans, sons and daughters of immigrants, the West Indians built a solid legacy. If the 1960s were marked by the burgeoning emergence of African intellectuals such as Kwame Nkrumah in Ghana or Patrice Lumumba in Congo, it has never been the case for French Africans. If the first and second generation of immigrants did have a more basic education, a shift operated with the massive waves of immigration which began in the late 1990s preventing the first generation from completing their experience, as we will explain it later in the book. As a whole, the African French never proved to be as efficient as the West Indians. Very active on the political scene, they were unable to build a strong political and economic structure, still invading the media spheres of their country. Plagued by the egocentric and manipulative ways and views of their leaders, they mainly organize and gather their forces around the politics of complaint, to either attack or deorganize to their own privileges and at the expense of their brothers dying in the ghettos and whose cases remain forgotten by the media. They are responsible for the decline in terms of intellectual criteria in the Black French community. Their parents, whom most of them never studied, were encouraged to immigrate with no qualification as they were exploited by the French government as factory workers. These Black African workers were used for their physical abilities and their arms, the French government being careful in not choosing intellectual Africans who could have represented a threat to the French White educated children prepared for the elite.

Profile of the Black French political leader

Just like Assa Traore, leader of Comité for Adama, the French-African politician comes from a dysfunctional background and is the child of these Black factory workers. This generation was born or raised in the French ghettos and has had a parallel life ever since, being educated within the association of toxic sub-cultures. He is, hence, a product of globalism. His identity is the admixture of a sub-Black Parisian ghetto culture mixed with the low cultures from African capitals to which a touch of Black

Americanism was added. These French African leaders lacked education, evolved in disorder and barely received the attention needed. These tragic blends allowed them to be the first targets of the left whose leaders never ceased to manipulate them. They have exchanged academic knowledge for a politics of complaint promoted by SOS Racisme and the Parti Socialiste. Hurt by decades of social exclusion, the *banlieusard* (name for the inhabitants of the ghettos) has a disproportionate relationship to power. A poor intellectual, he does not think and has proven to be unable to focus on the future. Though partially aware of his limitations, the associative leader needs and wants control. Therefore, the Black French leaders can prove to be as violent and brutal as any White colonial agent from the past. Consequently, they need emotions and have learned how to take advantage of it with the finest skills.

Selectivity

The Black French political leader is an elitist, yet not bright for being way too emotional. Though African in roots, most aspiring politicians are not truly concerned with their own kind. Indeed, their activism is a tool used at achieving social elevation. Thus, they find themselves to be selective when it comes to their indignation. They love and worship the elite even if corrupted. Limited in thoughts, the leader is barbaric and brutal in his approach and this peculiar trait makes him an easy target for the White leftists. Yet weak in nature, the leaders have the consciousness to pick and choose their models. They never cared for the struggle of the poor Black Peruvians or Black Ecuadorians, for they were born and raised in the poorer spheres in the world. Peru and Ecuador do not have any political weight in the Western sphere. Therefore, the lives of the diaspora, there, can not be capitalized. On the contrary, the African-American condition is easily marketable. Indeed, the Black Americans have heavily influenced the world culturally due to their incredible creative and intellectual skills. Yet, contrary to the Black Peruvians, the African-American was born and raised in the most powerful country on earth. If Peru was the dominant Nation, they would have used the pain and suffering of the Afro-Peruvian. The final quest of a French-African activist relies upon his obsession with power, not with justice and equality.

ON MARKETING BLACK RAGE

Profile of the French political leader

Just like Assa Traore, the female leader of *Comité pour Adama*, the French-African political figure often comes from a dysfunctional background and is the child of a generation of Black factory workers. These young activists were born in the French ghettos and have led a parallel life ever since being raised in the association of toxic sub-cultures. They are, hence, products of globalism. Their identity is the admixture of a Black Parisian ghetto culture, the low culture from African capitals to which was added a touch of Americanization. They lacked education, grew up in dysfunction, never had the attention needed and were the first targets to be used and manipulated by the Left, Parti Socialiste. They have exchanged academic knowledge for a politics of complaint promoted by SOS RACISME and the Parti Socialiste. Hurt by decades of social exclusion, the *banlieusard* (for inhabitant of the ghettos) has a disproportionate relationship to power. A poor intellectual, he does not think and proved to be unable to focus on the future. Though partially aware of their intellectual limitations, the associative leader needs and wants control and is ready to do anything to seize it. He thus has no shame in exploiting his own community. Since the Black French are privileged in their struggles, evolving in a country allowing them to express themselves in any circumstances, they realize through their experience that their condition seems better than many other Blacks in the Western sphere, thus preventing them from playing the card of oppression. Therefore, if they can not exploit the issues they claim to face on a daily basis, they have no shame in importing other issues which do not resonate with them, to accentuate their anger. The orchestrated protest by Assa Traore in June 2020 in front of the TGI in

ON MARKETING BLACK RAGE

Paris illustrates our point. Traore had no restraint in manipulating the murder of George Floyd deciding to associate it with the death of her own brother Adama, a criminal convicted more than ten times. No one there even tried to compare the two cases to evaluate the legitimacy and veracity which would unite the two men for being overwhelmed with sensations. Consequently, the leaders need emotions and have learned how to take advantage of it with the finest skills. George Floyd and Adama could never be compared for they were two Black men with separate backgrounds both socially and politically. Assa Traore, like many of her peers, made a mockery of the Black Panther ideology. In fact, Black people from the Western sphere were made the insult of the many ideologies promoted by their predecessors. If the Panthers were against capitalism, those who claim to be their descendants became the new slaves to capitalism by using the pain of the people to promote themselves and to become new leaders. They do not cherish the work of the Panthers in truth but are attracted to the glamour and image marked by the Panthers. The protests organized by the new generation of activists are not spontaneous but rather fall in between a conscious capitalistic form of marketable

ON MARKETING BLACK RAGE

Black rage. Emotions generate views and chaos could elevate any incompetent leader. Capitalism in the Western sphere reinforced the desillusion and the ego of the Black leaders. They are still privileged enough to choose their battles unlike their ancestors who had no other choice than to bow down or fight in hiding. One regularly enjoys the chaos and pain endured by the Black community as a whole hoping to say the right word which would seduce the spirits of the emotional individuals so as to have their own space to become a new leader. Finding a solution through building would prevent any of these manipulative Black French leaders to take advantage of the situation. Actually, none of them would exist without chaos and rage, for rationality would imply education, intelligence, dialogue, hence forms of well-being most are strangers to. The obsession for heroism or the complex of the "Black savior" is also another heritage of capitalism. It is the last step before the elevation to power. Using the suffering of the people to elevate one's self is corruption at its core. In this sense, slavery and colonialism exposed the Black leaders to a distorted relationship to capitalism and money. To fill in the void left by years of rejection and oppression, the Black leader is dangerously looking for power before justice. He wants to be a god and worshipped as a savior. He would never brave the danger of death an African rebel would face but would rather fantasize about it. Capitalism made the Black man in the Western sphere, an arrogant, depending, proud, emotional being with no efficient political strategy to propose. In any ways, whether pro-Black or not, once he reaches a new level, the activist will too become a part of the establishment and join the White leaders he once hated. His rage is another form of hypocrisy and another language through which he begs for being recognized by the dominant White entity.

Trans-Blackness

Globalist policies do not only affect life on a political level by molding a world after one model. They affect *africanness* as a whole. The parents who migrated in the 1970s to work as factory workers, never transmitted their heritage to their children who grew up tormented and lost. Ignored by the White French powers, the specificities among the immigrants were never highlighted but rather reduced to the maximum. The Malians, Senegalese,

ON MARKETING BLACK RAGE

Congolese or even Mauritanians became "*Black*" or "*Afro*". Hence, Black populations deprived of their cultures to become lifeless "people of color". This element preceded the destruction of the *Français de souche* or White French native, now deemed an enemy by the Black leaders who made the mistake to exchange their French traditions for economic wealth. In this turmoil, the two categories mirror each other for they both lost their essence to globalism. Through this absence of cultures and roots, the Black leaders adapt their identity to what one would call "trans-blackness", "*trans-négritude*" or Blackness with no frontiers. This limitless condition allows them to pick and choose, exploit each other's condition for the sole purpose of suffering and create a fusion within the diaspora. This, however, totally differs from the solidarity between African-Americans and Africans from the continent as we witnessed it through the actions of the Black Panthers or Malcolm X. These movements from the 1960s, were however, genuine. Today's relationship is the new marketability of one's experience disguised under a common social cause.

The Black French leaders excell in protesting, complaining and never at building any structure. They are actually scared to face this inevitable phase.

Building would force them to face their own inability to act as real politicians, if they want power they are not capable of organization. They opt for a false revolution being at ease with the idea of being co-opted by foreign forces. This presence reassures them. Without them, they would be lost. A good politician needs to prove to be efficient by building a new structure. They are, therefore the adult babies needed by the White leftist powers and supported by their brutal militia, the ANTIFA.

Manipulation

Why would the left find their allies among the Black French? Actually, the left is a brutal political entity. But they are the guardians of the colonial legacy. Leftists are deeply racist and reluctant to promote any Black politician at their table. Like the conservatives, they deem Blacks to be beneath them. This mechanism goes back to the colonial times. Each colonial group and powerful entity invaded Africans with their own mentality. If the Belgians and Dutch were closer to an Apartheid regime, the French were more invested in their conquests. Seizing the land was not

enough. They were more interested in colonizing the minds of the Africans. During the years of French dominion, the colonial power managed to create a relation of codependency, leaving the colonized entities suspended, waiting for a validation which would never come.
The Black French leaders use rage and revolt as a masque to dissimulate their true desire to be accepted by White powers. If they can not be aknowledged by them, they will hate and turn against them. The right wing powers are deemed to be the sole oppressive enemy when the left perpetuates the manipulation of the Black living in the ghettos. Weak in the

mind, the Black man sees the White left entity as genuinely kind, friendly through which he can find a mentor who could understand and validate his most despicable actions. In France, a young Black boy from the ghetto with a tendency for murder and crime will never be held accountable for his actions, for the left, with the support of a corrupted branch of other Black leaders, would always defend the criminal way of life, opting to use the racial argument to prevent any other individual from criticizing the actions of the culprit.

ON MARKETING BLACK RAGE

Distorted Vision of Reality

Political manipulation made Black French the enemy of reality. Since they ignore who they are, having been stripped of their roots, they do not know there to place themselves in the world. Though adult in nature, their mentality is rather reduced and manichean. The French-African activist wants more than he can actually build and take. Spoiled and ungrateful, he lives out of touch with reality and never knows when to stop. He focuses on power and remains indifferent to the chaos that surrounds him. The quest of power dissimulates a fear of

blackness, a fear of being forgotten and facing their own demons. The militant is a scared child who stands unable to face the consequences of his decisions. He is, consequently, incapable of living without the support of a group. He needs more anger and support when at the top, but needs someone to blame when failing.
The distortion of his vision flows from the denial of his own condition, contrary to the West Indians who descend from slaves kidnapped hundread of years ago. Sons of abducted peoples, they were never asked to come. Their existence and life was interrupted but the spirit of resistance never left them. The Haitian Revolution of

1805 illustrates our point. Yet, the French Africans remained on the continent and found the reason of their existence in Decolonization. The African immigrants and parents went from colonial subjects to weak decolonized individuals. In other words, they never possessed their destiny. The West Indian slaves had to witness their lives falling apart but slavery motivated them to seize their future by any means necessary. The French speaking colonized and African subjects were always scared and submitted to the French institutions. Instead of focusing on seizing, they taught their descendants to wait for the validation of their selves, through the eyes of French people. These African parents were responsible for the demise of their children, for they never encouraged them to possess. Therefore, since their parents led them to a slowing pace, the obsession for power is wrongly thought to be an alternative to the void they fill inside. Yet, the left mocks their inability to see things ahead of time. The French Africans refuse to aknowledge the disaster of their demise and this denial marks their downfall. No matter how hard they protest and yell to seize power, they are ruines, lost and frightened individuals deprived of a strong identity. They are dispossessed in nature and manifest this intellectual poverty through their disorganization. If France is a racist country in its institutions, the Black French were one of the most privileged African communities in Western Europe. The isolation in the ghettos was never unchangeable. Therefore, the Africans had one honorable solution to survive politically and economically by becoming full French citizens. Co-opted by the left whose members found perfect people to exploit, the French-Africans were progressively abandonned to their own fate, sometimes promoted as a form of wealth. Becoming French in culture was believed to go against Blackness when most of these association members ignore history. Western Europe was always in contact with Africa and Black politicians ruled the region for 400 year with the Moors. With their short and limited vision, the presence of Africans is only thought to date back to colonial times, while Black people have always been there. Blackness was wrongly made to replace identity and culture as the epitome of the condition was found among the African-Americans. The Black Americans are unaware of their roots and had no choice but to construct an identity based on their skin color. However, the French Africans can not survive on their own since they have not built anything. Dispossessed from the very first day, they were destined to be human failures, exchanging their sub-cultures for others, forming a new kind of destitution. The Americans, though copied by the African French, never neglected their citizenship for Africa, for they built the United States and kept following a logical pattern while the French blocked and tried to convert it to impose their own distorted vision. French culture was rich, with a language and a large literary heritage which was as acceptable and respectable as any other. Though proud of their Blackness, the French Africans are mocked by the

Africans of the continent who consider them to be lost. Yes, the Africans do protect their knowledge and roots.

ON MARKETING BLACK RAGE

Conclusion

France deals with its share of racism but the discrimination can be changed. The Blacks were privileged and less exposed to the disdain Black Belgians experiment on a daily basis. Their spirit of complaint flows from their feelings and is opposed, in nature, to the veracity of history and experience. Therefore, it is illegitimate. The privilege of legitimacy stems from the principle of law. Indeed, it justifies the authority of power of one dominant entity over another which remains submitted and always evolves around the relation of two individuals, for it implies the perception, the judgment and the validation of one's fight in order to reinforce the ego of the leader towards the exposed and despised individual. The average French Black activist is a traitor to his own cause. Though politically engaged, his actions are rarely honest and sincere. He became the mockery and the product of capitalism itself. He does not fight to survive for his resistance follows a pattern of robotic mechanisms. His goal is to be seen and worshipped, using and exploting spritual and social suffering so as to elevate himself. There lies his marketing genius as he lusts after the idea of power in itself. In this sense, the pro-

Black individual has become the oppressor of his own people and the first person to ever betray them. Recent social events linked to police brutality have proven to reveal a profitable market in the explotationg of one's community.

The new leaders have no profit in seeking solutions but would rather encourage the politics of complaint rather than building so as to move forward. This would expose their lack of efficiency in being good leaders. The obsession with "saving the Black community as a whole" is already obsolete for the phases of a global world are taking place and will annihilate any form of togetherness for Blacks in the Western world are no longer Africans but corrupted by money. Therefore, they would support any body with money. In fact, Blacks are the first victims of capitalism whose members entertain the capitalistic obsession. With public figures such as Beyoncé and Jay-Z, the Black community is doomed with the birth of a new corrupted elite though acclaimed by the new generation. And so, even if they built their careers on manipulative tactics, the exploitation of their own and the firm representation of the establishment.